SIGN OF THE TIMES

Peter Brookes

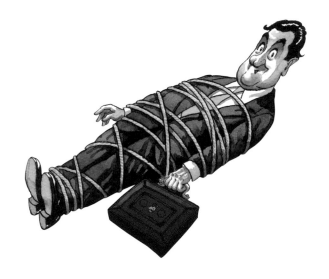

The Robson Press

For Angela, Ben and Will

First published in Great Britain in 2013 by
The Robson Press (an imprint of Biteback Publishing Ltd)
Westminster Tower
3 Albert Embankment
London SE1 7SP
Copyright © Peter Brookes 2013

Individual illustrations featured in this book were first published in *The Times*.

ISBN 978-1-84954-597-6

10 9 8 7 6 5 4 3 2 1

A CIP catalogue record for this book is available from the British Library.

Set in Chronicle

Printed and bound in the UK by CPI Colour

Introduction
By Peter Brookes

So here I am, it's four o'clock in the afternoon and I'm staring at a blank sheet of paper. I've been banging my head on my drawing board for two hours, chewing my pencils instead of lunch and still no bloody idea. Panic stations. If it doesn't come soon, I'm a dead cartoonist. Then, hallelujah! It's there, although it's been dragged out as reluctantly as the truth from a politician.

Only three hours to complete it. Initially I render it loosely in soft pencil, then I overlay that with pen and Indian ink, and finally I add tone with watercolour. How you draw it, though, is just the mechanics. The idea behind the cartoon is the tricky bit and what I wrestle with for the best part of the day. This begins early morning with the *Today* programme, progressing through reading the papers, attending morning conference at *The Times*, and digesting more news bulletins before the headbanging begins.

Achieving a likeness is an important part of the process. Take David Cameron (*please* take David Cameron). Was there ever a more Tory face than his? I draw the oval outline first, starting with the high and wide forehead, and drop in two circles of white for eyes, like two poached eggs in a pan. Add dots for a seasoning of pupils. His complexion is blemish-free and as smooth as a baby's bottom. I'm sure he polishes his face as regularly as he cleans his teeth. It oozes privilege. The nose is aquiline and patrician and the mouth tiny over a Mr Punch chin. His hair, if not an Eton crop, is certainly very public school; it's got bounce, and you can almost smell the Molton Brown. There is a definite quiff, and the parting has been known to veer from left to right. Perhaps it is a political weather-vane, but I suspect it moves just to confuse cartoonists. I complete him by painting circles of red, with white highlights, for his rosy cheeks.

The Deputy Prime Minister presents more of a problem. Nick Clegg's most distinctive features seem to be a permanently down-turned mouth and eyes in pools of darkness beneath anxious eyebrows. Not a happy bunny. His boyish, sometimes spiky hair and that put-upon air make him the perfect fag to Cameron's head boy in my coalition public school cartoons in these pages. I'm sure he would have made the not very interesting but safe choice for your daughter to bring home. I bet he played hockey.

Ed Miliband became Wallace for me as soon as he won the Labour leadership, with his geeky, hapless persona and cheesy, big-toothed grin. Something about the starey-scary eyes, too, and the nerdy way he stands. Anyway, the green tank top, brown trousers and red tie could have been made for him. Ed Balls invariably appears as Gromit but in a more brutish and leg-biting mode than the original. I realised the cartoons were touching a nerve when the Miliband team hit back in the press, insisting Wallace was 'a man of principle ... a great British hero'.

Some days I might want to be angry, in which case the humour I use tends to be black rather than comic. Other days I might want to be just plain funny (I hope). Either way, I follow no party ideology, have no 'agenda' and try to react to news events on my own terms. Whichever party (or coalition of parties) is in power, I deliver a good kicking when deserved. I am the 'permanent opposition', as Sir David Low put it.

All high-minded stuff, perhaps, but I frequently end up asking more questions of myself than I do of politicians. I'm a mess of contradictions, really, in a confusing world, and probably the best that can be said of me is that I never turn in a cartoon at the end of the day with the thought, 'That'll do'.

The Gaddafi family attempts to flee from Libya to Algeria.

RAF servicemen who fought in the Libya campaign lose their jobs.

GOING OVER THE TOP, 1914...

GOING OVER THE TOP, 2003...

A report on the death of Baha Mousa condemns UK soldiers for treatment of detainees in Basra, Iraq.

Vladimir Putin admits to stage managing animal stunts while David Cameron warns bankers over bonuses.

At the Liberal Democrat autumn conference Nick Clegg tells delegates that the party is punching above its weight.

Sarah Palin announces that she will not run for President.

Libyan leader Muammar Gaddafi, who refused to hand over those responsible for the 1988 Lockerbie bombing, is killed.

Nick Clegg announces who will receive proceeds from the government growth fund.

Amid the eurozone crisis, Greek Prime Minister Papandreou calls off a referendum and refuses to resign.

Italian Prime Minister Silvio Berlusconi announces his resignation ... almost.

NATURE NOTES

Hornbill
(Bunga bunga)

A prodigious little breeder, but with no hope of survival. It is adept at seed dispersal in forested areas. Often flies undone to keep its pecker up.

Fig.1

The hornbill is resistant to the call of the Merkozy Euro tit.

12 xi 11
Peter Brookes

Berlusconi officially resigns.

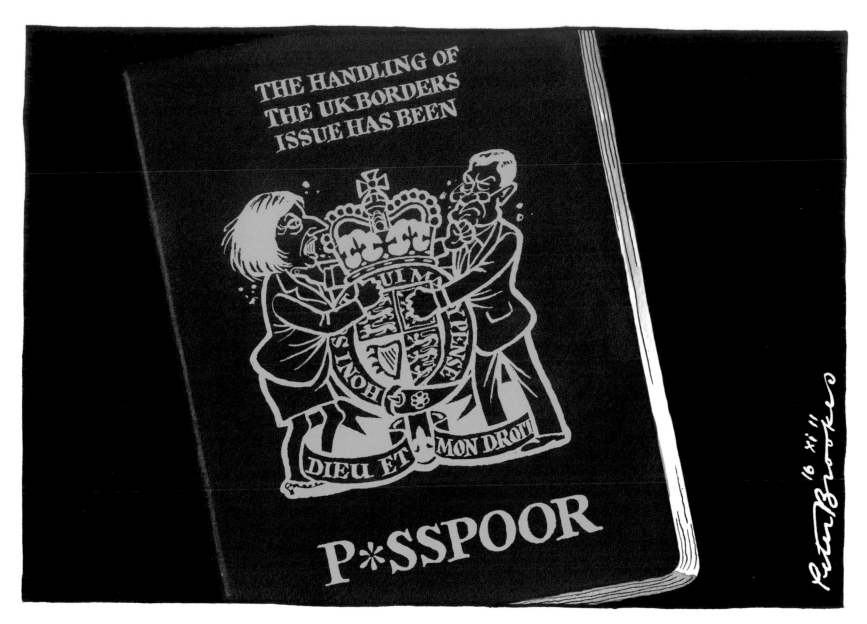

UK Border Agency head Brodie Clark is forced to resign while Home Secretary
Theresa May is under attack for relaxing border entry standards.

David Cameron vetoes a new EU Treaty.

President Assad of Syria continues to slaughter his own people.

Questions arise over Scotland's bid for independence.

A video of US Marines urinating on Taliban fighters goes viral.

Bishops in the House of Lords attack parts of a welfare reform Bill.

Ed Miliband delivers a speech in Glasgow condemning bankers.

Cameron stands by Health Secretary Andrew Lansley and his NHS reform Bill.

Lansley continues to defend the NHS changes despite growing opposition.

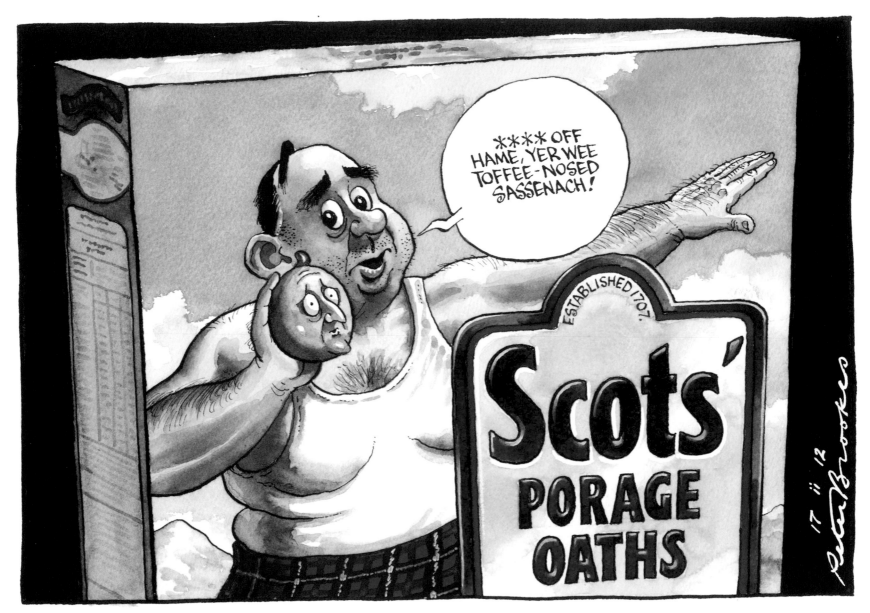

Cameron visits the Quaker Oats factory in Scotland and meets Alex Salmond to discuss the Scottish Independence Referendum.

A eurozone bailout of €130bn is agreed for Greece, but doubts over the country's economy remain.

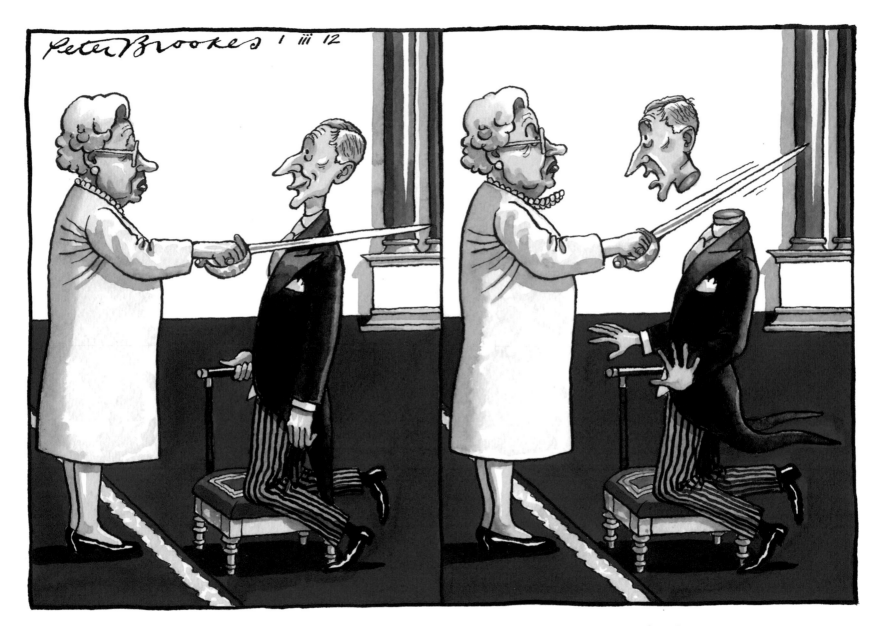

Fred Goodwin is stripped of his knighthood for his role in the collapse of RBS.

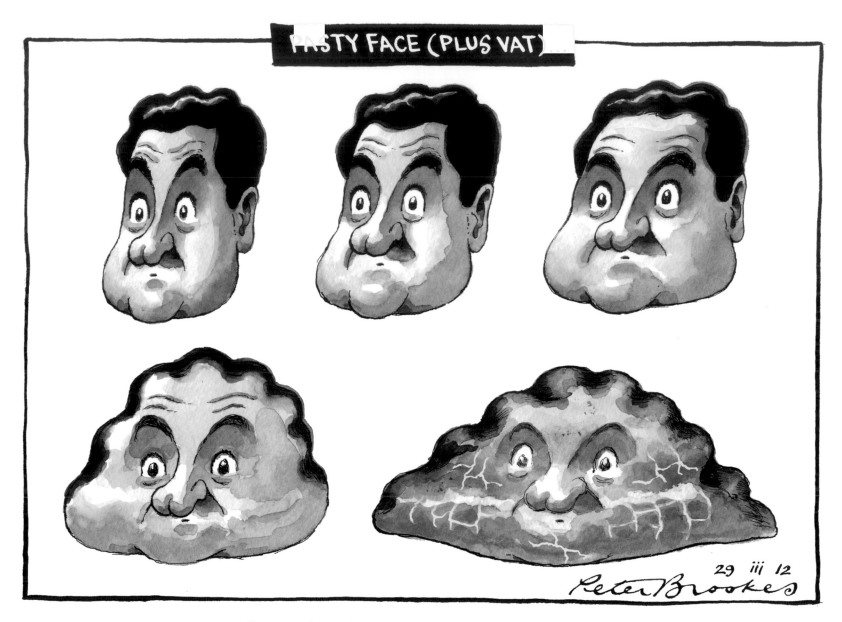

George Osborne is criticised for his proposed 'pasty tax'.

Cameron declares himself a 'pasty lover' and is also accused of hosting dinners in Downing Street for big Tory donors.

Bernie Ecclestone insists the Bahrain Grand Prix will go ahead despite bloody anti-government protests in the country.

Marinc Le Pen, leader of the National Front, refuses to back Nicolas Sarkozy
in the French presidential elections against François Hollande.

27

Theresa May is criticised as queues at Heathrow continue to grow.

Newly elected French President François Hollande meets German Chancellor Angela Merkel at a summit in Berlin.

Facebook is floated on the stock exchange while the Greek economy continues to struggle.

IMF managing director Christine Lagarde tells George Osborne to lighten up on austerity measures.

A surprisingly high number of witnesses are called to the Leveson Inquiry.

Mitt Romney, a Mormon, becomes the Republican nominee for President.

The Queen takes part in an extravagant 1,000-boat flotilla on the Thames to celebrate her Diamond Jubilee.

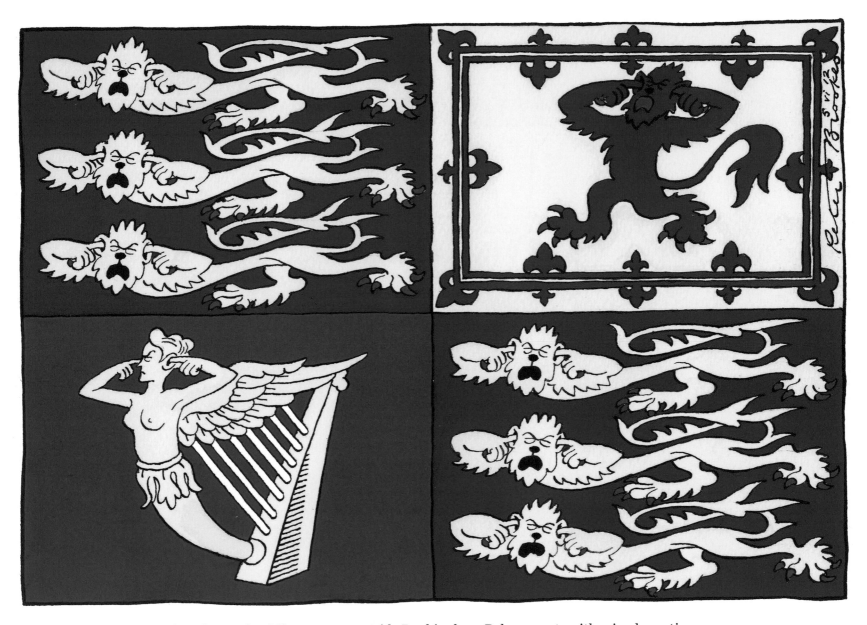

The Diamond Jubilee concert outside Buckingham Palace meets with mixed reactions.

Cameron faces pressure from Bank of England governor Sir Mervyn King and Angela Merkel
while James Corden wins a Tony Award for his role in *One Man, Two Guvnors*.

The G20 meet in Mexico while a UN summit on sustainable development takes place in Brazil.

During her tour of Northern Ireland the Queen shakes hands with former leader of the IRA Martin McGuinness.

Merkel and Hollande hold talks on the eve of a crucial EU summit considering the fate of the euro. (Nora Ephron died on 26 June 2012.)

Defence Secretary Philip Hammond announces significant job cuts to the Armed Forces.

The coalition government announces a £9.4bn railway investment.

Rules of the Game

1. Beach Volleyball
Two fingers means blocking your opponents and telling them to go take a running jump.

GER €

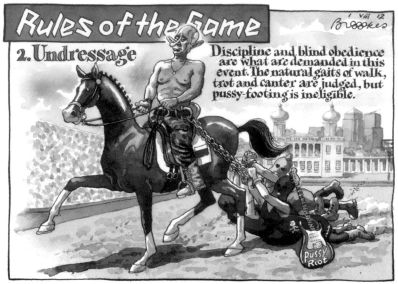

Rules of the Game

2. Undressage
Discipline and blind obedience are what are demanded in this event. The natural gaits of walk, trot and canter are judged, but pussy-footing is ineligible.

Pussy Riot

Rules of the Game

1 Launch into jump
2 Attack apparatus
3 Perfect landing

3. Vaulting Ambition

Rules of the Game

4. Men's Double Skulls
Overwhelming force, muscle and aggressiveness will help you win the day. Orders are given by the little bloke behind you.

The London 2012 Summer Olympics.

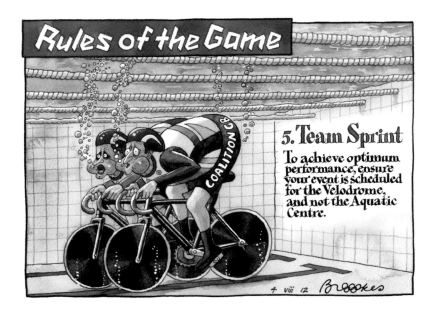

Rules of the Game

5. Team Sprint

To achieve optimum performance, ensure your event is scheduled for the Velodrome, and not the Aquatic Centre.

4 viii 12

Rules of the Game

6. Foiling

❶ En garde

❷ Allez

❸ Arrêt

❹ Riposte

8 viii 12

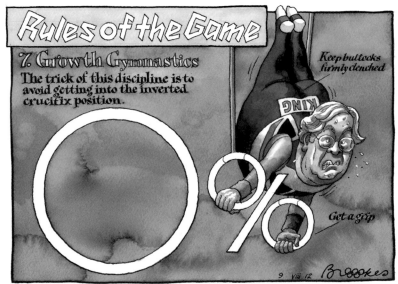

Rules of the Game

7. Growth Gymnastics

The trick of this discipline is to avoid getting into the inverted crucifix position.

Keep buttocks firmly clenched

KING

Get a grip

9 viii 12

Rules of the Game

nit Creek

8. Canoe Endurance

The objective is to stay the distance on a brutally difficult course, without the shirt on your back. And no paddle.

10 viii 12

Education Secretary Michael Gove announces that GCSE exams are to be replaced by the English Baccalaureate and the remains of Richard III are discovered in Leicester.

Ed Miliband declares that Labour is the 'one-nation' party at Labour conference.

The Rothko vandal is arrested and Boris Johnson gives a popular speech at the Conservative Party conference.

Allegations that the late Jimmy Savile sexually abused children and adults are widely publicised.

George Osborne gets caught sitting in first class with a standard ticket.

The electorate seems divided in the days before the US presidential election.

Obama is re-elected, the Syria conflict heats up, riots continue in Athens and there are more public hangings in Iran.

Justin Welby is announced as the next Archbishop of Canterbury.

David Petraeus resigns as director of the CIA after having an extramarital affair with his biographer.

The Leveson report targets the press but omits any mention of social media.

George Osborne slashes the welfare budget in the autumn statement.

The House of Commons hotly debates the gay marriage Bill.

Cameron gives fracking for shale gas the go-ahead.

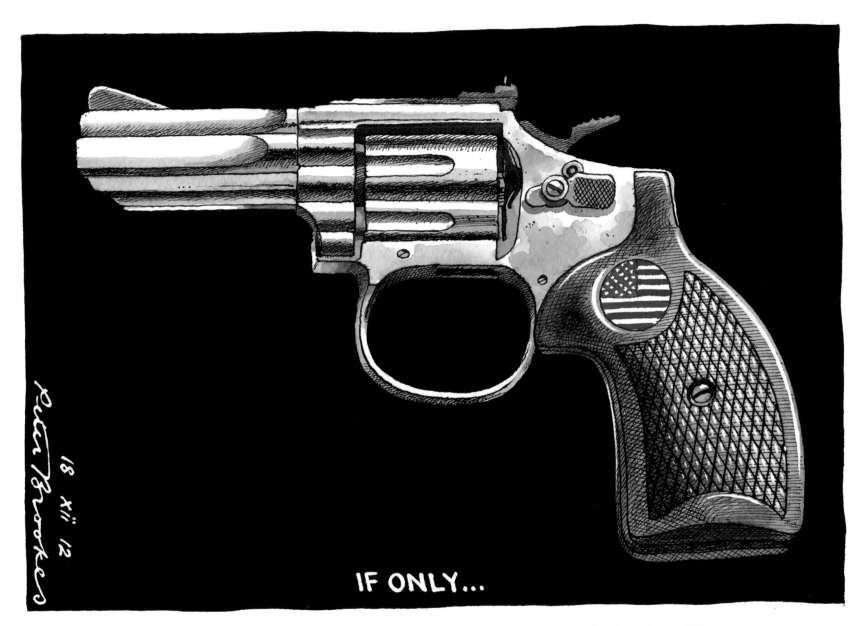

IF ONLY...

An elementary-school shooting in Newtown reignites the gun control debate in the US.

MPs vote to cap increases in most working-age welfare benefits.

Nick Clegg admits to owning a onesie on his call-in radio show.

NATURE NOTES

Swivel-eyed Toad
(Ukipus farageis)

EUROPE

Habitat: Not here

Fig.1 Screwed

UKIP £

Reptilian creature, with a dry, warty skin and a penchant for squirting poison all over the place. Hates frogs.

Support for UKIP leader Nigel Farage increases.

60

Cameron faces a tough speech on Europe.

The horsemeat burger scandal rocks the UK.

David Cameron promises an in/out referendum on the EU.

Nick Clegg suggests the coalition cuts were too deep as GDP figures indicate the economy is approaching a possible triple-dip recession.

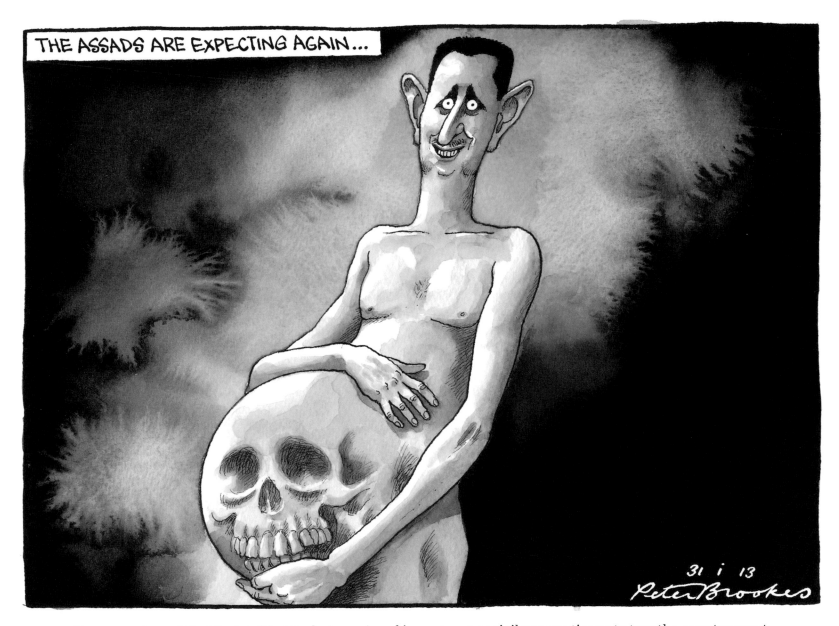

Rumours abound that Syria's First Lady Asma Assad is pregnant as civil war continues to tear the country apart.

Nick Clegg makes a resurgence as he continues his 'Call Clegg' radio show and prepares to fight the Eastleigh by-election.

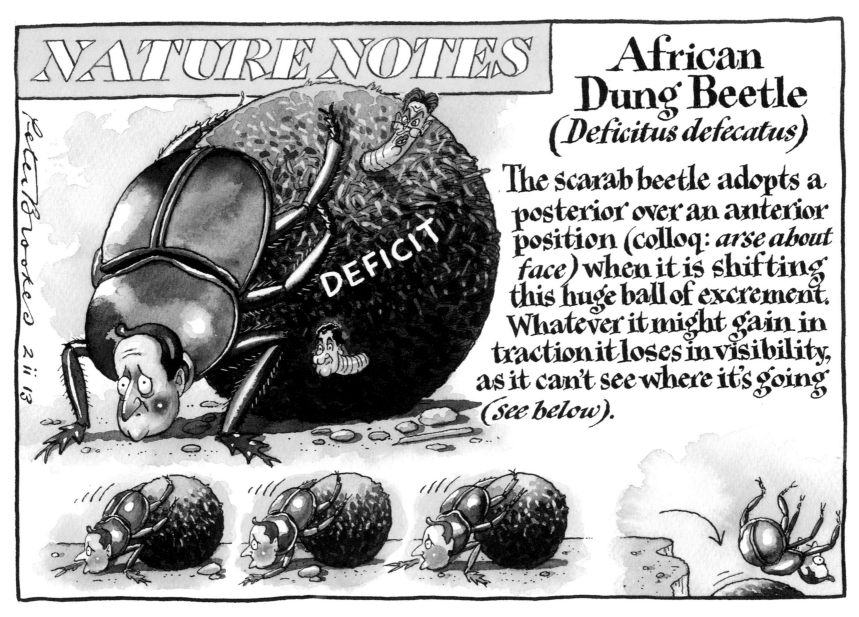

David Cameron faces criticism for confusing debt and deficit in a speech.

Chris Huhne is convicted of perverting the course of justice after transferring driving penalty points to his wife Vicky Pryce.

Cameron and other senior Tories reiterate their backing for equal marriage despite opposition from within their own party.

The EU makes the first budget cuts in its history as the horsemeat scandal continues.

Pope Benedict XVI becomes the first pope to resign on his own initiative since 1294.

North Korea stages a nuclear weapons test in defiance of bans.

The horsemeat scandal continues to make headlines.

Author Hilary Mantel faces criticism over comments about the Duchess of Cambridge.

The Pollard report, which looked into *Newsnight*'s decision to drop an investigation into Jimmy Savile, concludes that there was no foul play.

The death toll of UK forces in Afghanistan continues to rise.

Problems stack up for the newly elected Pope Francis.

Cypriot MPs reject the terms of a European Union bailout due to a controversial bank levy.

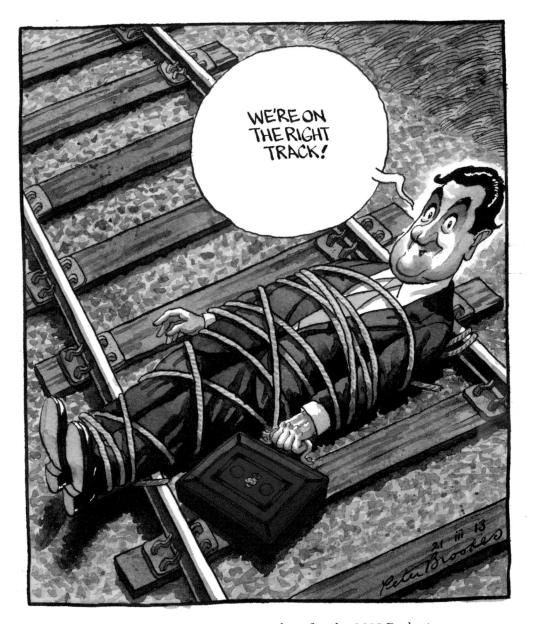

George Osborne announces plans for the 2013 Budget.

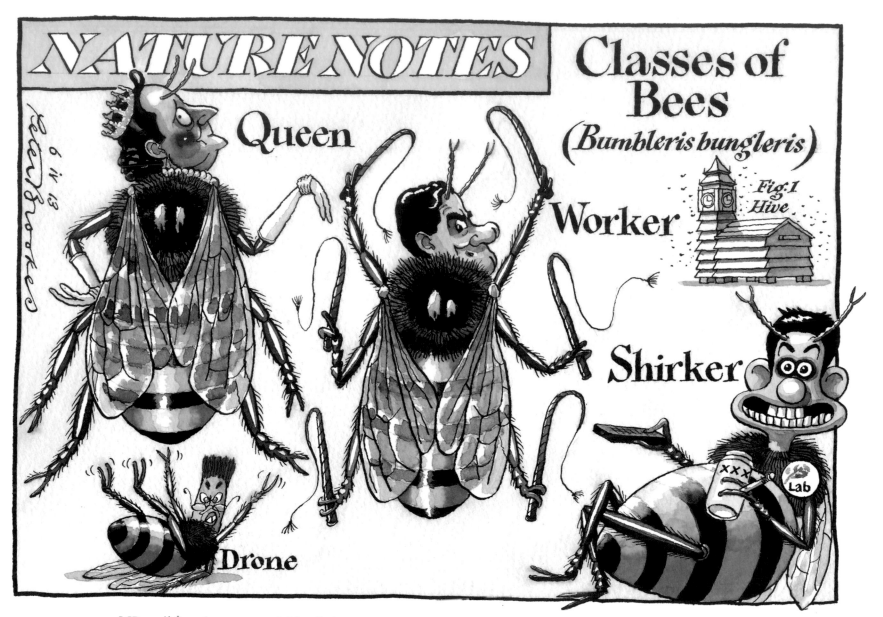

MPs call for a ban on pesticides linked to bee deaths while the debate on welfare reform continues.

Former Prime Minister Margaret Thatcher dies.

The press speculate over the shortlist for the Turner Prize.

A memorial library for Margaret Thatcher is announced.

Ed Miliband receives a ribbing after his turn at the Scottish Labour conference and renowned graphic designer Storm Thorgerson dies.

Boris Johnson's brother Jo Johnson is appointed head of the Prime Minister's policy unit.

David Cameron admits that the Conservative Party needs to be more diverse.

UKIP do surprisingly well in local elections.

Nigel Farage welcomes former Chancellor Nigel Lawson into the clown fraternity.

Sir Alex Ferguson retires as Manchester United manager.

Commander Chris Hadfield performs 'Space Oddity' from the International Space Station as Cameron pushes for an EU referendum law.

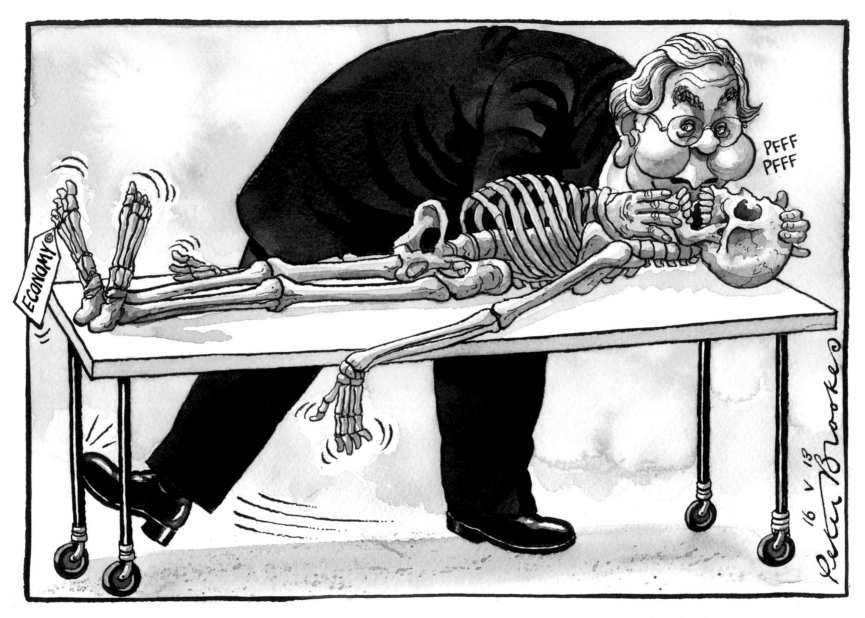

Sir Mervyn King delivers his final economic forecast as governor of the Bank of England.

Nigel Farage is mobbed by Scottish Nationalist protesters in Edinburgh.

MPs continue to debate the gay marriage Bill.

ALEX SALMOND LAUNCHES ECONOMIC CASE FOR INDEPENDENCE...

Google boss Eric Schmidt delivers a speech defending the company's tax arrangements.

Ingrid Loyau-Kennett is applauded for confronting the Woolwich murderers.

Fighting and mass murder in Syria continue under President Assad.

The cash-for-questions scandal rocks the House of Lords.

THE BLIND LEADING THE BLIND IN IRAQ, AFGHANISTAN, LIBYA, SYRIA... *Peter Brookes* AFTER BRUEGEL

8 vi 13

The UK and its allies consider the possibility of military involvement in Syria.

Abu Qatada faces deportation from the UK while Cameron debates arming the Syrian rebels.

Mohamed Morsi, the democratically elected President of Egypt, is ousted in a military-led coup.

Union chief Len McCluskey declares he has lost faith in Ed Miliband.

Andy Murray wins Wimbledon.

Tony Blair backs the military coup in Egypt.

Samantha Cameron urges her husband to tackle the Syrian conflict.

The Lib Dems reignite the debate about the cost of Britain's Trident nuclear deterrent.

Spain challenges the UK over the sovereignty of Gibraltar.

The US uncover an al Qaeda terror plot and author and academic Mary Beard is sent a bomb threat on Twitter.